Travelers Leaving for the City

Ed Skoog

Travelers Leaving for the City

Copper Canyon Press

Port Townsend, Washington

Cover art: Dan Witz, *Econo Lodge,* 2006. Oil and mixed media on canvas, 46 x 32 in.

Copper Canyon Press is in residence at Fort Worden State Park in Port Townsend, Washington, under the auspices of Centrum. Centrum is a gathering place for artists and creative thinkers from around the world, students of all ages and backgrounds, and audiences seeking extraordinary cultural enrichment.

LIBRARY OF CONGRESS CATALOGING-IN-PUBLICATION DATA
Names: Skoog, Ed, author.
Title: Travelers leaving for the city / Ed Skoog.
Description: Port Townsend, Washington : Copper Canyon Press, [2020] |
Identifiers: LCCN 2019043451 | ISBN 9781556595813 (trade paperback)
Subjects: LCSH: Murder victims–Poetry. | LCGFT: Poetry.
Classification: LCC PS3619.K66 T73 2020 | DDC 811/.6–dc23
LC record available at https://lccn.loc.gov/2019043451

98765432 FIRST PRINTING

COPPER CANYON PRESS
Post Office Box 271
Port Townsend, Washington 98368

www.coppercanyonpress.org

Acknowledgments

My thanks to the following publications for printing poems from this book, some with different titles:

American Poetry Review: "Tarentum" and "Tumbling After"

Cortland Review: "Travelers Leaving for the City"

Critical Quarterly: "Clayton's Friend from Back Home Who Came to the City to See Widespread Panic One Halloween at the New Orleans Lakefront Arena, Disappeared, and Then She Walked By the Pizza Place" and "Unfinishable Sentences"

Gramma: "Timothy McVeigh at the Dreamland Motel"

Harper's: "Night"

The New Yorker: "Pittsburgh"

Poetry: "Guard? Guard!"

Poetry International: "American Football"

Virginia Quarterly Review: "Love Is Like an Itching in My Heart" and "Slender the Residence of Immensity"

Deep gratitude to Carl Adamshick, Jeff Allessandrelli, the Attic Institute, Catherine Barnett, John Beer, Rachel Berrington, David Biespiel, Malachi Black, Victoria Chang, Heather Companiott, Matthew Dickman, Michael Dickman, Craig Florence, Thomas Fox Averill, Anne Gisleson, Shauna Hannibal, the Idyllwild Arts Summer Writers Week, T.R. Johnson, Ilya Kaminsky, the KPals, Rich Landar, Mark Lane, J. Robert Lennon, Ben Lerner, Kelly Luce, Ray Mann, Jill McDonough, Eric McHenry, Susan Moore, Lonnie Ohta-Mayer, Gregory Pardlo, Elizabeth Scanlon, Zachary Schomburg, Sophia Shalmiyev, Rich Smith, Justin Taylor, Elizabeth Urschel, Kevin Young, Matthew Zapruder, and friends who hang around Mother Foucault's Bookshop. My enduring thanks to Elaina Ellis, Alison Lockhart, John Pierce, Michael Wiegers, and the rest of the staff and supporters of Copper Canyon Press. Thanks for the memory of the poet Derick Burleson. Most of all, my love to my father and brothers, the Marquis family, and Jill and Oscar.

For strangers

The Pittsburgh Press, February 7, 1955

GUNMAN FLEES WITH GIRL WHO REJECTED HIM

A Homewood man was shot to death today as he stepped between a young waitress and her enraged former boyfriend. The killer, holding the girl as a hostage, fled with a companion in an auto as police converged on the scene at the Lang Hotel, 7048 Frankstown Ave. Walter "Whitey" Henry, 43, who lived in the hotel, died in a second-floor hallway moments after the rejected suitor pumped two bullets into his chest from a blue-steel revolver. Police identified the gunman as Russell Winterbottom, 33, of 257 Braddock Ave., Turtle Creek. Winterbottom is missing, along with Miss Lorraine Rodgers, 20, of the Lang Hotel. Struggling and screaming, she was pushed into a two-tone gray auto parked outside the hotel. The car sped away before stunned witnesses could get the complete license number. His parents said he had been distraught and "pacing the floor" ever since Miss Rodgers left him in early January.

Contents

THREE

Travelers Leaving for the City

ONE

My Shirt

                    I grabbed
        the shirt off the hook

on my way out into the night
and bore it past the
            cathedral

where a wedding was
    being
swept up and offered it
                    to the man
falling asleep against the embankment

he said it wasn't his and
        waved me down the
                alley
            the shirt made a face and wanted me to
        wear it

I said maybe in the
        morning then as the rat chattered under the
                car

        in the Pre Flite Lounge I
set it on the piano and hurried back toward
        my own losses,
    keys alternating
    with shadow a white
of a parasite bird's
        hunger—and on the wind I

    heard the silkworms
a thread maker   a tailor
telling me that around the
        corner

a horrible infant would be
calling my name,

and was, only it was the emptiness
        of generations, and a vine
coming unglued from a downspout

        so I had to remember
  suddenly the password
that lets and lets and lets
until there is no more
        permission,
  silhouette
    imprecisely bless
each footstep with
                light rain—

Travelers Leaving for the City

where does the starting happen at

before.   unbeginning scroll
    before the set of disagreements   language of the shoot-out
which is language's unscrolling
    nothing specifically human about the heartbeat
a crumbling wall

        they put away their light duffels in the rooms
they talk about the labor of dinner, divide
    into pleasant domains the onion chopping
corner-swept bedmaker

        following an idea long clapped and retrieved
        quick walk around the pond, a bleak
deadeye of when memory will falter

        dusk between leaves

        a breaking into the eye

        the way back's cyclopean

    and unstoppable, I need to be
            ripped gently apart like a thing
        with gears

and I stayed, stayed, stayed quietly
        with bliss of supper and play on the carpet
            before bed. And I tried to make sense

and make meaning and make money and
masks, and I have deer on my side instead
        of hunting, and the rolling of dice instead
of their enumeration

a painted bell, a portrait
that rings. And watched the scroll in museum
light, static, and coursing.

Watched day develop
all in one person, the many-personed self,
heat in the shade, the long sentence
waiting for the doors of granary to open,
dragonflies by the pond

the garden and the wild
rough drawings behind it, and I am working
my way toward dying in my own surround-
sound increments

Farmers at the waterwheel:
the massiveness of the farm in their shoulders,
angle of the bucket

the weight of the cooperage,
that's where the beginning, spilled droplets
in moth-littered dust. Even before we met,
we never got over each other. Over you,
and the composite blue. Winter does when
we are together things

All at once the congregation
gives up, sells the bell, sells the sleds. The shale,
and the shadows of the shale. Leaves you

walking from the chapel to the train
livid with sleeping bags and wet couches
we never get over each other, in person.
Past the forms and the farms

past quarry and query.
    The moon's flesh and the river's an ink stain.
    Under the bridge they step out again,
  argue with the pallbearers and the brides' pallor.
    The birdseed and bindweed. They stop for milk
  around midnight, and get me some hot dogs too
  while you're in there

I'm not going in.
    Where am I suddenly. Oh, the land of the dead pardon
me, I didn't realize it, and the letter said they
    aren't going to be delivered
are they. I had thought
  the audience for these moments was an ear
      like my mother's ear

but now I see slip
    galleons from the edge

She Said She Took a Train

but there is another thing

I went down to the rhododendron field
because leaving for the city
                    she heard the pots and pans

                    there is a way of being
alone ghosts know
        a trick
to ignore what you're aware of

        rowing out
                    dawn's fishing boat
        into recombinant weather
                            or rowing in
            with the tide

back to shore

        there was a lot of weird stuff
in my pocket yesterday
            now where is it

the ring of water
    her iced-tea left on the deck chair

she said she took a train

        I suppose she did
                her compartment
fabric coming apart
            like a coconut shell
                    sitting up to half-sleep past country
smoke and factory yards

she moves through city toward him
like a product sent away for
its weight
side-shifting in the hold

she took a cloud
I suppose I took
cloudiness
and fix up my own
apartment with borrowed money

break toy box into liquor cabinet

crack sunlight
and you'll come over and drink steeped tea in soft chairs
while tallow burns a kitchen window
to frame approaches
and midway through
sleep hear the mouse addressing
itself to doorway
fix it all up
with bartered time and roast
chicken in wine you brought two springs ago
with rosemary
sprigs
one for the chicken

one kept in the shallow
of a water glass on a side table

I will be the one who hasn't forgotten
fixing up

apartments as
treatise on finding
one's corner
the overhearing

Pittsburgh

isn't there anymore

rode by it
on the gray horse and instead
a place where they go sick

a place of only mist

To properly understand the twelve
Pittsburghs of the heart

but nothing to grasp or die for
and when the adults told me to cry
I sang on the uneven riser which swirls
like northern lights in the ear

In 1955
my mother's father, a steelworker
was shot and killed in his hotel

intervening in an abduction attempt
the shooter "crazed and lovesick" according
to his mother
my mother only met her father
a few times, the last time
shortly before the murder, she said
she took a train.

In the testimony of another tenant
his face, after he staggered
out of the apartment, burned "an iron color."
He fell into her arms. "I was
holding him, trying to help," she said.
"But he was dead." The kidnapper
escaped with his ex

and they drove the outskirts of Pittsburgh
      Tarentum, Aspinwall, Turtle Creek
all night
before she talked him into turning
   himself in at dawn

          clouds are in a composition useful
to fill space around the invisible
         in moonlight the murderer
and the owl who buries and the bull who rings

    drove rural Allegheny County

stopped at midnight for hot dogs and milk
      according to the transcript
of the trial
   heard the luminous
processes of the dashboard

I suppose he sang
      like a scarf
   gone out long behind
   like magnetism

      like thornbushes

   like wind
around a highway sign
   he went up and
   asked if anyone was dead again
      why they need to
  assert themselves
even after we told them about sorrow
      think my grandfather's ghost   rode
 alongside them eleven miles

peering in
   before departing

who wasn't with him the night he was killed

like hearing a stranger's headphones
in the spirit of canceled flight and a storm coming
                    she missed
the beard he was growing
                                        we put our gods in clouds
                    we hide in clouds

Tarentum

                              then the mouse who ate
the moon left the cheese who was so

alone it made a movie about loneliness

   it doesn't matter

how reduced her fingernails were

bitten and chewed
                how red
the lipstick on the cover of her lap's
movie magazine the couple sold
at the station
              him high haired and priest-eyed
         and her in a blue scarf
laughing when he tripped on his broom

oh, lost again on earth in hallways
where repeating doors never close my eyes

I am forever waking in sheets and in bare feet

feel my way along the wallpaper
to porcelain bath
         green soap
         a curved
story that brings me back to mattress
when I wake
         stretch
                    my mother was born in Tarentum
         elephants
invaded at Tarentum

Horace wrote about Tarentum
                        ornate
        the hotel we sloughed off

when we missed the train
                                had to rouse the hotelier
whose key was chained heavy
to a dictionary

                        rode elevator up
                                himself half
            asleep

                        I slept on
floors in that property of vapors and liturgies
                cold outside but the heater
too high updazzling with murk

                                        encountering it
                I miss the train
over

                        over
                I am trying to keep   my appointment but get lost
on the vine

                        in the giant's cloud
                                a vast pneumonia
                of course the vine
wanted to grow there
                to suspend
between two fires a trembling
thread which when struck
shudders with vision
                tangled by what god

        the wrong date on my calculator

the wrong frame around my self-portrait
    while she traveled her mind along rooked streets

2.

I reach with you into Tarentum

where once nothing lived

    an ambience congealed
    brussels
sprouts rot in the calendar

    asparagus rises early

    late
summer we smell the olive groves
before we see them
    a splendor
that predates memory; even in date groves
where palms in estrangement tower over us
we may feel the vegetable pull in each sense

you can live if you wish in Tarentum
    e-mails circulate through the company
    reply-all notions of meeting
    promotion

the boss's emotion concentrated in casual;
some language misdirects
    heads down
the wrong broadcaster's breath

its bread-and-button
                nothing ever goes
wrong here
                I can't believe

                                it's the hallway again

                as one with a fever
but perhaps not a body

yet wash
                wash the body
                with a song
in the eyes
                beach towel around the knees
                                daubing the undershoulder
                last

the water drains
                draining the hour
I can't read
                repeat then
                what are they
going to make up to explain

Tarentum is also called Taranto
                                I rise earlier than my hosts

set out exploratory for their
neighborhood
                but the block *hath no endynge*

lion-pale lawns set out for dummy

      crocus in a graverobbery walk miles
through early sunup
        the residents
      still in night's pullover
          it is
      as though
I am not anywhere
      the regressive wind
through fingerbone branches

although no tarantula lives near Taranto

the tarantella was first danced in Taranto
to diffuse the poison
      so if you're bitten
around Taranto
      know it's where the family's
from of Quentin Tarantino
      if you know   movies
      if you duck into the movies

on cold weekends
      on other walks

other times
      through subzero streets of Mankato
a town I don't know
      even the bars
I duck into are unfamiliar

as a kid in Topeka when it was
under the highway
                    across gravel
to go over the Burlington Northern slurred
                                    coupled
            at night the sound
came into houses of Greenwood and Woodlawn
            sat down
                                        ate onion soup
            mornings
faster
            afternoons you could climb up
ladder
                    over the handshake
            and down to the river
            color of a banker's shoe

always carrying a little life
            little death

but I also see a chain-link fence   reflected in a puddle

                other puddle reflections

                            places where puddles dry up

in stages
            the cracks written there
            the flakes

the traces
            It is
            as though someone took
a rock
                    smashed the back window
of the moment

the way Donovan and I shot out the back window of a police car with a BB gun

      what was I keeping
there
    for later

4.

    the butcher at Walter's Grocery glories

  he hasn't killed anything
      only made
cuts here and there

      a dot of blood on his sienna mustache

    I walk into new
shoes

       I head to the hotel again
           like a beautiful stranger coming down
the street carrying very little
    to not meet me

I saw a screening of *Jackie Brown*
        on Aurora Avenue in Seattle
  we were a test audience

           Tarantino was there
    his long
black coat was there
    some of you

already dead
    have known more than
the sash cord which I know is tied
behind the panel to significant weight

                              in older homes the cord becomes
spectre-thin
            and breaks
                  few people
know how easy it is to slip screwdriver
into wood to open the side door

slip new cord through
                  tie
                        like fishhook
my cold numb fingers try to knot on the shores of Duck Lake in
onrushing snow

            seal it up
            like a mausoleum

but what has really been pawing at me
                        like a neglected companion is the concealed
                  heaviness behind simplest
      surfaces

                              how most of the time I have
no idea how to begin repair

people are blown away in movies, Tarantino

none of us is long here
            but most will make it
through

                  night's where the constellation
is that I'm looking up at from the yard

      Orion probably, his molossus belt

                  my grandfather was blown away
                        became one more unmoored figure
in the fading star map that spreads

over my city in power blackouts
                    looking up I tell my son he should see
the very old things in the sky

let's go inside
            he says
            but stay
in the front window where I can see you

                        for now that's where we are

on either side of the house's plate-
glass cataract
            the window sliding up
                        sliding down while the weight
does invisible work in lamplight
                    in starlight imagine one another

no leaves where my grandfather's body
was remanded blow away
        Military Cemetery in Pittsburgh, haven't been
            all memory
of him except this poem has blown away

                        5.

because the rabbit is a filament in its bulb
because the child has to hear three
stories every morning
            because this poem

if you hold it up to the wind

                    he is a filament in bed
        I'm a rabbit in the field

long leg
                    constant nibbling stupid

stupid
          stupid
                    outside the field

I'm not sure there is any meaning
                              like what you catch in the window
of an ambulance in transit
                    or a parking
space interrupted by a tree
                              my grandfather wasn't blown away
in Tarentum

          lion's forehead
pressed into my sentence what is better
than books I said
                    what of the structure
of the hair
                    the suggestion roundness
gives of the earth other
                    says
there is another lion at my liver

          asks of us again
          grandfather is
a dead language called Tarentum

what yesterday showed itself
          as a snake

today arrives
          as cloud

they take you in
            in a bouquet
of last year's Tarentums
            returned
                  as a flowerpot ache left
            returned
                  as a secret then secrecy turned car
around again
            I've never been there
                  I'll never get out

The Lang Hotel

What if
I am the shooter again
    rustling up stairs,
        where will I put the gun this time,

    which hand, or half in a pocket,
or tucked into waistband, under the shirt

      In one dream I find the vine again,
    this time the orange butterfly lands
        breaks into chrysalis,
gray then green as the leaf stem
      and when the caterpillar emerges, thorny
and ravenous, I turn to the mirror,
        wake

before what I see begins to speak the book
I wake holding
    often, and my name is

      four-paned window, with a shutter
figured in the upper left, a kind of chute
          howling from the upper right
    bars below it, and in the remaining
        quadrant
a circle, or a ball, or the letter
    that begins my son's name but oh,
so many other enunciations also

even after you're shot
  a photographer continues to shoot
    the city that rained on you as a child
and a series of your lovers
    your beds and floors and attics, speak back

the lens has a leg and a drug

such a drag when they shoot you
    and the photographer's busy at the mills
which are silent
        but the wind comes through in shifts

        manufacturing a kind of steel inside your chest
when you try to move

the faces we sold ourselves
        and the hunger we cooked

A rabbet joint supports a window frame
    a door, cases for books and stairs

    your movements make poems in the air
people are starting to show up

            Tomorrow is the man just leaving
again ask me
    what I'm sure of
Sun's broken, heart is one word
    stars in bloom
dust clouds shadow
        a frolic on the lawn

Friendship Avenue

a photograph by W. Eugene Smith of a
woman in a maternity dress waiting to cross
the street, or for a bus to arrive, beside a stone
wall at an intersection a nearby sign says is
Friendship Avenue

I.

If in the essay of her hands
the hammer
      and the sign of the hammer
         I could hand down
because the ledge was not finished

We were still hauling the supplies
      in backpacks and on stretchers—
        inch through the door as you go—

    sent ahead of the hotels

      both uplifting,
like lids of eyes and caskets

     ashes within ashes
       the intimidating absences
    then in what
tonnage

the series of explosions would detonate
    in what eternal coil
if only they found one another
   father on one hand
       their distance opened
decades before the shotgun blast

                    opened   chest

like treasure
                    and on the other hand

daughter, my mother
        always then a traveler, a going-on alone, into spaces

where the construction was never joined
unfinished
                    parts of the house

                    like the void
between the roof and the walls
    or the closed-off room
                    animals get trapped in
    you can hear them scratching but can't quite place it,

        cats know, or you dream of entering
—an animal dream space
                then, closed with leaving,
how immense, the waves that push through,

        oceans pour through, within us.

                            2.

                    I remain—ashes within ashes... Whatever
                    else, this past week ended the Pittsburgh era
                    of attention, whatever else... yes... whatever
                    else, and whatever is the residue from its
                    trials and from its failure. So let us ride with
                    the sign of the crossed fingers. (W. Eugene
                    Smith to a friend, June 28, 1958)

3.

       I'm talking
to you
         grandfather
         for the first time and it is so quiet in this essay of her hands
you can hear me

         as hummingbird   hears honey
           I don't think I can help you
up from the hallway floor with song
              the impression that reading about you   has given me

         like thought arisen
while reading a travel book
         vivid spires and dusk-lengthened roads to forested
         realms that I'll never see
         even if I went
             as I cannot go to you
         nor any word about you

no word would have been kind
but net to catch unintended trawl

               as the residue of gold intrudes
most normal of basins
       and conjured your figure grinds out

they sing something I need
about silence
        as pertains to love
        and now will turn vine back through lattice

              as a garment floating uneven down
              ripple and shadow
        a blossom
frozen in falling

a flower shop
opening infernal drunk rigors at dawn
                ray undulating
around the sheller's finally fanged
                mushroom fire

4.

when was it
you first knew you were or were not dead
                        in the hallway
            or on the kitchen floor
while the cockatiel squawked
or noticed only its own reflection
in birdcage mirror and nothing outside

or woke from dream unsure
                your path
through the world might just be a free trial

an ultimate technique   the figure

        like a disk

without space or time to commodify it

I think instead is full of slides and trapdoors

a ladder
        a song
        don't wrap it up

I'll take it home in the essay of my hands
            even though
we are down to one lane
            what does holding
the disk which is a void make you forget

the trick with wheels for
                    the meters run out
                            even the star map
                    infinite presents
a figure that parceling into titles may wall off

  match the wood to the old wood
                    scrap what's instinctively not part of the design
they sing it this way
                    use the words
about the loss of the figure who would explain
the bark
                    a sap
                    a pith
                            leaves

        bright fall
                    and how it is to see the nests in winter
                    and how it is to smell the burning forests

        their
                            ash running away from the mountain—
the absence of what we thought mother was and father was
                    when we were small and needed and cruel

Tarantella

Time's the thing that's not the mind or the baby

time's a baby in a sling
        a minor electricity

water and dust
        a kind of suet in a hanging cage
                is larger than whatever the universe
    turns out to be (a strawberry pip) all tough winter

which has been shown to prosper

seen from the past the line is the present
                when the
      astronauts came back
      bid us bury
  our gravity
          grow the lines
that are the story of loneliness
      waste

either enough or not enough

  I walk past potted plants in the side alley
        marigold
     sunfollower
     a good plate

give a little water
      adjust the moments
            constellation of last images before sleep:
a walk around the drained reservoir

arrival at the island: having a theater
all to yourself
and they show the movie anyway
through the present's glass-bottomed boat

I see your traces in afternoon transit

unmemorized now pull up
the song and in every room call out
for me again
in awning and trestle
the forty languages of dust

small
tigers fill silence around the moon with scrap
salaries of the engineers

until we're tuned together
like each
string on the first guitar or any string figure

loop and knot
that tells our story
over and over
unraveling
It's a clear line
I want you & when I say that or the sun

blot-hearted
bouncers check ID
like birders searching
binoculars for plumage
and in the alternate-day
parking a portent

like an off-year election
upbraids the lightning sky
I'm the glow-in-the-dark screwdriver

stabbing your collarbone over and over
                but that's lox
for you
                flayed and secretive on the morning
        look
                I don't really
know about my grandfather
                who died
long before I would have
                                not known him

                Round
        was the dish of mints in the conference room
        where we signed over my mother's liver
                        some mints soft and pastel

some hard with white covering
        mint grows back in the creek

        the liver grows back too
                        largest organ
                no not *skin* mother
        skin is *on*
        the body—we addressed this
        with the host at trivia night
no
                not the one I go to each Sunday
with friends
                but the constant one

TWO

Timothy McVeigh at the Dreamland Motel

You must tear yourself up entering room 25,
the way children were torn apart
blasted in the day care, and it seems I must say it
over and over to myself, that he intended to,
that he intended to kill the children
and not see the killing, and took pains
to avoid being hurt himself, who was once
a child & got away, as one survivor tells
how pinned beneath concrete so tight
she couldn't spit out her gum, she held
an unseen hand disconnected
and although the detail is grotesque
she said it was still part of the real
person and I am holding your hand
into the smoke to be changed by events,
holding my own child's hand at crosswalks,
in parking lots, in public places where danger
is disorder, a break in the pattern
that conceals us like a snail in its shell,
which delicacy is strongest, slug or snail,
a metal slug is a round bullet, it spins
like a planet, in, bringing the morning
Timothy McVeigh rose and slept,
just like you and me, and if there is a soul,
had a soul, and if there is no soul, had no soul,
and so it is with you, who doesn't want
to read about Timothy McV
any more than I want to write
about him, but here he is, striding
toward the getaway car the moment
there is a blast, and don't you feel
waves pushed at you in that sunlight,
how it cleaved the day? He got only
so far without license plates, pulled

over for the infraction and caught,
when enthusiasts talk about freedom
of the road, that distance is part of it,
the highway miles he was nobody,
like the midnight roads the murderer
of my grandfather rode before turning
himself in to the police. You may be
allowed to tear yourself up like a ticket
entering into the world of bombers,
the explosive avenues and rigged doors
and want to turn for peace to beauty
as a badge, that you might be known
for your goodness. Bless the dead. He
registered for the room as "Bob Kling"
but tore it up and put his real name,
he talked the manager down to twenty
bucks a night instead of twenty-eight,
the Ryder van may or may not have been
parked there, still it is uncertain what
happened, in what order, as often
the case is when the sluggish estuary
of language washes into memory's
current. My real name is Ed Skoog
but I dreamed another name which is
a window, with a window inside it,
and a ladder, and a ball, and two arms
reaching, and because I drew it once
and tore it up, and threw it in the fire
I tear myself up when entering a room
with a poem in it because a poem is
meaning, and whenever you pay your
twenty dollars and step into the twenty-
fifth room there is a poem on the table
which is too horrible to read and read it,
the one hundred and sixty-eight names,
the words for their lives, I have seen them,

their photos on a grid, but in the room
I lie down on the carpet and dream them
also, they are dreaming and wake up,
shower their bodies which certain traditions
say are just the vessels for the soul,
and they brush their teeth with assorted
toothbrush styles, the toothpaste brands
they have come to prefer, they shave,
they comb, they protest the comb,
they go downstairs and have breakfast,
they run to the bus without breakfast,
their lunches are packed, they are planning
to go to lunch. They are government
workers, they work for the government.
They are the children of workers. The
children are learning new words each day.
In Junction City the voices are waking too,
the clerks and the neighbors, the owner's
son who tells the driver of the yellow bomb
he can't park it by the swimming pool,
only by the sign, the taxi driver who said
he didn't give him a ride, and then okay
he did. The bomber peeled back the plastic
of his ID and burned the paper, and the next
day showed it to arresting officers. He ate
a fruit pie. He is throwing the wrapper
straight on the ground. They are weighing
buckets of nitromethane on a bathroom scale
out by the lake, they are slitting open
the ammonium nitrate, they are pouring
fuel into barrels, I am mixing the racing fuel,
white fertilizer pellets turning bright pink,
and seal them up, affix the blasting cap,
connect the long fuse. I do this every day,
I wash my face, I brush my teeth, I wash
my hair with antidandruff shampoo,

I cleanse myself before stepping into day
and coax my son down to breakfast,
I am pouring cereal, I am pouring milk.
We talk about what dreams we had.
The Dreamland Motel's been razed,
its iconic sign installed at the museum
in Oklahoma City, brought inside
to light a room with its neon star,
its Vegas lettering. The movable letters
read *Welcome*. The bombing fell at Easter.
He was executed a little after Lent
with intravenous drugs, then
one part became president
and one the fight against it,
the same as day that covers the memorial
bloodless and bowed. It was bull
shit that drove him to do it
and the same nobility he claimed
to feel is inside the language now
I am using, this sentence has a fuse,
you must tear up a poem that you
enter, and the sound of the tearing
rhymes with allowance and defeat,
he had a poem read at his killing,
one that has given comfort to many,
he was comforted by a poem. Torn
and burned, drowned, thrown far,
the bombing victims worked for the
government of the United States,
they died working for it, and now
a days half the time I want to give
up and say deal's off, the thick mire
slog to be is too slabbed to brain,
asleep in room 25, the highway loud
and the bombing practice at the fort
nearby tender in lullaby thunder,

the pillow thin and spring's menthol
drifts in the open window, prairie
insects legging the screen, lacewing,
blister beetle, medicine moth, flesh
fly, bombardier beetle, and the false
bombardier beetle, which has no bomb,
and when I wake I may still be there,
the terrible truck outside, and even then
and this is what facing the ghost tells
the dreamer, what the false bomber sings
to its cousin, I may walk into the hour
keyless, into the last minute may step
toward the beautiful cowardices of love.

Clayton's Friend from Back Home Who
Came to the City to See Widespread
Panic One Halloween at the New Orleans
Lakefront Arena, Disappeared, and Then She
Walked By the Pizza Place

She said the show was still going on
    when she left
        in a wedding dress

    echoing coliseum behind her becoming
    a moon
            as it disappears and instead
    a departing music arrives under her bare feet;
        palms grow acres above
  confetti in her hair
        she said *human*

        before I can
pack up my tent and go
      how does
last night learn morning or it's morning

time develops
    as any interview will

           and sometimes string music will turn and enfold
           you in its uncomplicated
    embrace

hear
      do you want to hear me
      I want to have   heard you the way I want the war
film festival to have ended
      program   folded and back pocket and reread
on the bus home

                    the interviewer's voice
        carries through the apartment

    I'm interviewing
    the streets of the city that led her
    without harm
            barefoot and veiled

over nail and glass shard and needle
                        the painter and I looked all night up and down river streets
            ungainly arms
tangled out of car window
            a little car   teeters on beady wheels
            carves the corner

an event develops

            like we're drawing
lipstick across the city's flirting grimace

people gather at intersections

                        as though the city knows she's gone

                        that was her who walked by
        okay

did she believe we searched all night
the houses
                        their secrets
                        the past
        writhed invisibly its visage
                        and where
                        a rider might come aboard one notices
        the birds differ
                        feather in a more
vigorous order

      as dunes refashion
the beach after a dream of searching
      each house for a bride
            bride one has
   always been
            paused at erotics of last
thought
         I'm here to kill some part
of myself with either exposure or a shroud and it may take all afternoon
         It will be
a daily observation
          a glimpse that will
    throw my reflection back
      like fish I can no more start over
      or start
new chain of interlocking construction
paper
      than I can begin my life again

or bring back dead
      somewhere
in the park's the fountain that makes you   make the same lesson over again
       as the bus driver swings down
    the lane in the snow
     and misquotes Blake

we throw off one set of snow chains and immediately put on another
  augural twenty-six or so letters that thrush
    our names from cities and corner town
       bars weird compositions left
to rust and grow
    long to become
their sons and daughters and grow
  long beard in hardware aisles
among boxed nails   a screw
    arranged by its bore
    from the bridge

a kind of voice
          wave that would become   the suit
       you know is hanging upstairs
   in all possible cedar closets

door open, window open

Tumbling After

Children move through the climbing tree

     like clock repair
until it seems
    the device is ticking
                  duration
is change in play
     though climbing takes
no time
     only one cruel as a parent
would measure it
     count down the leaving time

                  as thought finds branching
    the rising
of the agent through feature is
     like   matter in gas state rising
     tunnels
in the air: that are dug operationally
          made by moving very simply through

painters on a scaffold: as we fall

they are building: forts
     from blankets and pillows
     words from sound and guess

time the pathway child takes through space
between branches
     without revision

path to fountain by quaking
     aspen   marigold

hold hands
to sprint through spray to where
the accordion functions
                    fumes

yet although it's nearly bread pudding
season
                when they
                ask the player to pause
his engine's junctions of folded paper
                    how much he's made

Now to get it wrong differently
                that's what no longer matters
                acrobats
        unwrap lean from pole top
                    spin
down widening rounds to land
        at the pyramid's foot
        repeatedly through the night
like a mother going back to bed

  My mask is whistling
            help somebody
    in the lost
                found where the good
        tippers power-wash the fat and ugly lines

                listen to us talk into it
        the game
personifies the rhyme
        so that rhyme
                    assumes character

or it is that the second
sound is the first's impression
        parody

            flat
                sharp
            I could jump off the roof
into your ear

            let's see if
            we can get into the lipstick factory

        change subject among foes
                    the low   levels rattling under eyelids
    I don't know how
        long: fly away Jack
            fly back Jill

    the boat is seething left at the library's
effortless
                    intertidal grief
                    a blue band   marks the highest water

  back notchless arrow
splashdown anthem lobbed between stones
                        banks are lending
        vast shipments bleed
    forth from ports
            state legislatures are
  buttoning their vests

            rising to speak

these children however
            after dinner-speak
            march in single file around the columns
                devour

what is in their path
        pretending

    only pretending

American Football

        the shoe
goes on my foot
       like a forest on a bear

            we eat with the crushed teeth of the middle class
           a diplomacy of lovers out for a walk
immoderately lost in time
      the dead move
          like cars with snow on them
        we learn it from our mothers
     who know
   that life is combat
       because they are women
           a tactic of the oppressor is
   get others to do its work
          becoming a racist was an important part
of becoming the oppressor
   but it was not the only part
          third squad of the eighth-grade
football team uncoached I observed

we beat up Larry O'Neal
       called him a cockroach because someone had seen a
   cockroach in the small kitchen
    of the small house in the corner of Topeka
  beside the plasma-donation center
      a urology clinic a house
the guitarist of the band Kansas
lived in for a while
   "Dust in the Wind"
the cover of the album
   John Brown from the mural

who would understand the dynamic
            that late afternoon of mouthguard and shoulder pad
            helmet instead of brain
                        white
            black and Mexican, native,
            we all had
a good time pushing Larry into mud
                        him getting back up
            I don't know
if they ever arrested whoever stabbed him
    in the parking lot of a Topeka bar
a few years later
            was it me
it wasn't not me in some sense
            that I was also
                        never Larry

in that I feed my masculinity
    every day with scraps
            or do I give it   my first bite
            the monster figure
would be
            ashamed and proud

    I thought
            for me not to have been
subject of the blows
                jeers this time
            and in a uniform
            the good people wilt
in the crystal vase where the fascists
    allow them to behave

Running Away

And they sing: I had a plan

        kept a green pack with selected

toys   flashlight
        a change of shoes
        only when
I
        asked if I could run away they said no
so put each object back where it brought
the house joy
        when it doesn't matter

some people are called lost
        but nobody's
going very far
        not with this gravity

not at these prices
        the fig tree is a strangler

cormorants in vile arrangements
  stagger the fallen dam
        I was a child I go around the houses calling out
names they   respond with various stratagems

  they sing our masks slip and in the yard sale
  everyone's a stranger
        to get through
  the day with your button you may

        need to forget what's disappearing and be like those among us who hear
        do your best to ignore what
even now is fading
        what falls
  outside your shirtsleeves

The Portland Water

the gasoline of mowing brings rosemary into the noon
children are picking their noses
telling each other
about skin color
and pretending their parents are dead

faraway   Porky   Pig
is peeling
wallpaper with a lotus egg

and the dog dogpaddles in his sleep
there is swimming in the river now,
some thrown rock sidesaddles to the bottom

suicides return in longboats
walk around for an hour
sun is working at its sunglass hut
an invisible escalator
running in my head is called desire
the river is piss and ag runoff and quilted
by a recurring breeze and deferment of a salmon beauty
no one swims all the way across that you hear about

out here where the gravel is
the mimosa's long feathery branches

with confectionary frill

tranquil in its dry way

out here where the gravel is
walled and unwalled

cities of grief, cities you hold

indifferent city

curbless streets potholed
　　down to truck, tarp-broken boat
　　　　the dumpster left over　　a renovation that faltered
　　crowds of teenagers are necessary
the shit they break needs breaking
　　out here where the gravel is

　　　　　　the world is a falling room
　　what sand thoughts my sleep
　　rolled me into　　curtains show

no draw, and yet night's shell
　　has broken open
　　my son, who'd climbed into bed

—where is he now?
　　　　not every night do I look down the ledge
but there he is, on the floor

　　　　and I am the one who lifts him
like a helicopter flying a bladder
　　from the lake to drop on the fire

I'm the fire, burning home
in the dark for anything broken or bruised
　　the shit they break needs breaking

　I stay awake and plan the day ahead
　out here where the gravel is
　singed and collapsing

Unfinishable Sentences

The world that for shorthand I call mine
        reassembles

    like glint on the prison chapel's
barbed wire   sharpening
      Only a guest

    farther up the June mountain
fire barks and thud
    down broke, then home
  past u-pick farm
      turning suburb, barn
      mid-demolition

  This is the deck the dead
deal from, the flower relaxes into itself,
as into a director's chair

  The forest buries its own
hill with smoke
    a father lost and searched for
 Closer to town's like a mind in rehearsal,
  going over the part

meadows turn into yards

and yet how the past
   sticks out
like a banjo's fifth string
     rude and pitched
      higher and on the wrong
        side, the insistent note
out of sequence, but if
  you like it you need it

And there is a rumored sixth
    string, invisible

Guard? Guard!

Tournaments lasted days and changed you
                                    but today the living and dead
speak through the microphone
of "I voted" buttons
                    erogenous zone

a place in the mind's wrestle

pause that votes and bets
                other voters   return to homes
        run dishwasher   read to kids
            get high and craft

still others walk golf course
turning gold with sprinkler

                no one   hangs who had not already
planned to hang at some point

I've thrown almost everything and broken within
                    activated
                                like a glow stick

        It is a sustained

throwing; an act with stink
of trash—power out—each evening

stair and light switch
            and a pause   unenunciated stair-structures
close off the switch from voice
to silence   this morning

            a snail
bore its huge garden shell

the color of owl into the afternoon   this time of year
    you can see the bottom of the lake

I set the excess down by the door

        near the fire   where the weather vane points
is where I'll carry my father slung fleece and steady
      footfall
into valley of brushstrokes

    crazed and smoked   enveloping   riders
        us
        trot-dazed in a conjectured
landscape paralyzed by the wind's chisel

clouds are a sheet the volcano staples
above parking lot to hill   where owners

talk on the last phones

        as long as the sheet holds
we will be darling
    or it is
the mildewed sail battened down
where we hide from fathers

light rain makes rooftops new   boughs fracture
    like lines
an iced-over pond zags ahead of a boot
        in there we glimpse inquiry

a hand goes up to stop the process

    folds this balloon into animals
    vehicles
a weapon

  the air inside song

or last breath   or first

     I'm a dog when I ape my words
        who would dent
or differ

     the teeth of the pig are it whispers red and brown

and recede now that they have
been mentioned

      when I look
close: not us
       this departure   hurries by and is
      like the lion

who simultaneously guards
the books
          elsewhere tests
the river with a paw
       stone in the first

              lean flesh in the other world

where the sun is blessing glide
back into thornbushes
           I am stone
      guarding stone
        It is no predator I would

   like to be

torn in half by
      from the logging road
a cut
     like a jeweler's work down
to the shore where sea stars disappear
leaving nukes

love metered and syllabary

     also the rocks
they used to cling to exposed
green clocks at low tide
     dawn's
a fishing boat uncertain past the rock

stone to touch
     chord on chord
     warped
sexual knuckle in flushed purple
          a hundred hues of orange

     offshore

THREE

Hostilities

Put the face of this fever
on a stick
              outside the theater,
   horrible goggle eyes
      red rimmed and its   mouth

 burned to beak
like a mad parrot
              The city sounds
   like an ocean
     both are excavation pits
furtive cadences   everybody going somewhere

    I used to go to group
cello lessons
      at the local college

    Kids with big cello cases
   trying to walk together down a hallway
            scent of resin recirculating in the HVAC

 To play cello you put your hand in certain positions
            the way rocks are
   rearranged each wave

       and for lunch you go to the same place
or a new place or you bring your own or you skip it

    The ocean is about hunger
   you look at it and think what could you eat in there

and its own indifferent hunger it eats people it eats boats

The ocean bows like a cello

the human voice like this, approximate
to someone like me talking
intimately to someone like you

But who are you get out of here

December

The cold brick patio as snow
calls its favors in

    is like my grandmother's gray hair falling
on the plaid collar of her winter coat
    when I'd hold her arm.

    From the botanical garden   hiss of steam,
      its tropics prospering behind tempered glass
and after the hiss I hear   memory
      of snakes in shadow.

    Once I saw a snake
swim up thin treble of creek
      rippling like commas. Time
    feels round now,
hoops to spend suspended
      and who was it

    stepped off the elevator
      out of the hotel through a side entrance?

    In the library window a couple studies,
laptops open, the clock
    behind them, a different time

    from what the antique coffinesque
standing clock says here
or what the carved hunters are saying to
    the cantering stag

    charging along the front panel,
  the guillotine swipes
left, right.   Snow
    disguises my rental car.

The stranger returns by the front door
carrying a different briefcase, and when he
      opens it on the plank above the radiator,
  it's summer.

Slender the Residence of Immensity

It frogs in from the front and fails.
Concentric broadcasts summit the senses
   and slide the faculty a sleeping pill

in midsummer custody
like spots caught midway up a giraffe.

The driving beard of permission
   perishes a legation into the coliseum.
   It's a legitimate

intimacy swept by the
greenbrier in a swivel chair
   but the lieutenant

gourmet's goldfish
   has gone unnourished again so has gone golfing
      blessed and blameless, bickering and salting.
   It's an uneven undoing.

The thrush shods.
   The peacock packs a peach in the possible parenthesis.
Heavyweight, the hearse crutches close
   the gazelles are enjoined. Extraordinary.
Such scrollwork from such eyeteeth.

      Hey Travis I'm at some bar in the Mission
         by myself and remembering last winter
   what we saw in Montana, stopped for gas
      as the first snow fell and we had to
         go around the mountains

      the three blue
barrels that said *deposit elk hides here*
   overflowing and even below freezing
      the death smell–it's stayed with me, Travis.

Thanks for help driving. Anyone else would have
    said too much about it.

Thought I'd tell you
  I was thinking about the invisible knots
   that bind together the part of the world
    I'm falling from to the end

either like a gutter
 in pursuit or the prey, the elk on the trail
   antler first. I want a late night with the wild
people who keep danger

taped to the inside
   of their encounters. I want to help them burn
down the company picnic

and remain
   in their heads to show to the beautiful lizard inside
 help with the parcels and the empties
   and the next day unchanged or even tired.

Love Is Like an Itching in My Heart

To wear a vigorous shirt. At See-See Coffee
    in the bathroom, a sticker on the hot-water tank
says *It only takes one or two*

seconds to become
helpless in flowing grain, or among flowering graves,
    down where the boats are being unloaded.
  It happens so swiftly that one

becomes another.
    The door opens and it's a new house, new knife
    and fork, new restaurant

by the railroad station.
    The wave crushes its salt, cloud into a cup.
  It saved your life once at a coast

pinstripe skulls
      and cherry-blossom smoke. Help me up hit
    me up hit me, while steamboats throw
  themselves at the shore

and low hills
  shag into farm. I'm a snap says the resident.
    I'm what there is about the dead beyond change.
  It runs out. How easy, the wave farewell.

      All along the way out was a New Year's kiss
    beneath a Supremes poster
  the daisy-decorated leggings
unfurled on the floor.

  She tells her boyfriend
    the boy who has been writing this poem
      ever since that night, that she was not dying
  it was all a joke, the trip to the hospital

the chemo
    all a lark that lasted an hour
a lark, so, to fly. I don't know if you learn anything
       about love from poetry, but you can learn about
    poetry from love

the way you can know a city
    from walking around it. The boy who has never been

    in love before doesn't understand and, never understanding
leaves the apartment, the Supremes
    the year of 1991, and the leggings

    rolled up on the floor like bird nests
      the body that was dying and then was not dying
but still shivered under sheets
when she came—the breath

    down the stairs that turned halfway down
   beside a flowering tree with a bird feeder
which in winter had pocked the ice-persisted ice.
     I love her for pretending to die
a lie of such richness

and for being able to die, both of us
    any moment, so that when I begin to, in whatever hour
      I may find it again
        that adrift sense
        that abandon, to be careless
    about the future again.

Car Door

The self is more than running
your hands through fur.

Take account of the birds,
the body, the sea, each departure

a tedium wrapped in a promise
and in that process the city where I am going

will rename me, as I'll rename the city,
a city that's easy not to see when you're not there,

easy to find when you're by the river in winter,
stepping onto the ice

in service of mystery
too heavy to haul home

maybe because I like the world
only as it is

broken and frayed
and the moment

when I feel what
may be pain, or relief

from pain and is
only something else

a note played on a body
as music may

mean only music
and the world only.

Then say night is a broken car
in the time of repair

when hard looks were like a door
open to the street.

The Rounds

Cut from the debate tournament,
I'm reading
in a houndstooth

coat on the stone fence between
the debate
Manhattan High School and the City Cemetery
plowed snow unmelted
with the last speakers drone stone what I'm reading through
persistent windows

cracked open drifting across the fence from their hound's teeth
new graves round earthen patches
and tanklike schools
speak through cemetery grass
where the small

plow was driven snow
persistent against cemetery gate it seems unmelted and obedient

youth on one side of the window, the graves cracked open on the other
a minor difference

empty, except for a few teachers' sedans
and buses from nearby districts, the lot
seems like a slate that could

dip into the flood of youth
and the landscape boulders
bushes
remain slate, shot through with earthen sunset
as if they have never been touched by water
or anything that appears and runs away

inside   layer after layer of textbook and poster
  would be cold to the touch
        if one passed

through and ran a finger along the names
beyond school, small houses

      that are always across from a school
          across daydreams of water
like a cold poster
          first bell runs away, the last bell is a ring finger
    and all the impatient
melancholy loitering
      applause after last arguments
somebody will have won, achieving trophy.
        It will need a goldish lacquer,

        and show a lectern
      and a figure standing at it, hand raised
small and breakable,
buttons on the blazer, lifelike eyes blazing

Topeka Nones

The alley behind my father's house
is like my father
  becoming weary in the afternoon
reading in his burgundy chair

  a yard dog naps
    in the silence before it wakes
to jangle collar like a jailer

    a blue jay calls after a train
both of them unseen

      like time and its freight
        layered in boxcars.

What is being carried through me?

        On the other side of the train
I suppose it's the river that's gray.

  Probable farms
      glisten.

    In the alley, the trash truck's mouth
      goes *maw-maw-maw*. Ants
row up the fence post and become

the golden saccharine of the honeysuckle.

The Long Hotel

I was going underground before I understood sex and death are both
    present in the lamb

who capers the meadow in perpetual surprise
    and clambers up rock-
face like a ladder

  until the sleepless farmer takes a lantern
      into the fields, listening for bleat, the power
that like a funnel through
crops would overpower
    the lamb, bound anyway to the city on a platter,

    and finds it torn apart in a cold scene like birth,
the wolves already scattered. The farmer takes both

      terror and comfort in violence become ambient
in the going-about, latent in stories wend
as consciousness can't be more than wind

    which roars the motorcycle helmet until the end
      of a ride through mountain's rye by headlamp
and the rider's outride of the life-warmed and worn

    life she's made in the young city
Down the rivers wend
    and flatten to seaside villages of fireplace sorrow
where each lives in drench,
      eagle to worm
      to postal carrier to visitor, whose visit dents

    their drier weeks. In cloistered bars they snort the powder
and outwait the dock-bound labor of the prow
      no ship will take them on, until the ship's their own

body ringing with the fearsome chimes of birth
and the low tide resonates the dreamers' breath.

On the bridge whose tensions both landings bless
the traffic twists. The trucks through commerce wend

but also solo walkers on mysterious errands: both
feel the girding rumble. In the hills, the wild boars
set tooth to moss. All this to say, dear, that the lamp

is broken and in the morning, I'll have to call my brother.
In coastal float we'll see what echoes from birth
rather than the fore-echo of birth's
answer, the long series.
At times I take the incoming tide like a serum.
And you'll let the tidepool simmer like a broth.

After storm, and the city's out of power
candles fumble on, and it is as though a birth

is occurring in the room, moony shapes appear
and the true nature of our
living is born, crisp as pear
cider we pour to wait for light like a wand

to pass back over our faces. So let's pogo
at the sex-and-death festival that's never over,

the free tickets we won for being the tenth listeners.
Then appliances churn and the moment goes slack.
I don't think I know how to outwit power
except the way the talon lets go in a sparrow

moment on the cherry branch. That quiet sugar.

Night

He wants the lamp on.
Night is a kind of work.

He says leave it on
although he is still

in a great way asleep.
I who am still asleep

leave on the envoy
who is always trying

to be turned off.
These murmurs

am even I aware of them?
The distance is

uninteresting
and the commercials

get caught in the webbing
of my eyebrows. Bring me

the head of Ed Skoog
again.

I am at the whale competition.
See me in the highlight reel.

Here is how you draw a face:
draw anything.

Famous Monsters

As the hand that holds the gun is a stone
diamonds are embedded in

As the wine pours cold into the thin glass
as rain slides along icicles

As wrens in bushes As when I say good
morning and they say nothing

As knives on their magnet silhouette
riders on the top of a hill

There are signs at the airport
there are signs

Always—the moment is always—and the dead step into it
as into a bodysuit   As into a shower

The Iron

My son likes to stay in hotels
because they have great pools,
but what I like is ironing a shirt
with the iron the hotel supplies
on the board that folds into the wall,
with the TV low, and whatever
weather is going on outside
in its most intense and local phase,
and what I feel in those moments
is both anonymous and myself,
not father, not son. My mother
was full of warnings about hotels.
One warning was never leave a glass
beside your bed, or you may fling
out your hand and slice your wrist.
And so I don't. But then my son,
back from the swimming pool, says
if you die wearing glasses
your ghost will wear glasses.
I like to take off my glasses entering,
then go to the window and look out.

About the Author

Ed Skoog was born in Topeka, Kansas, in 1971. He is the author of three previous books of poems, *Mister Skylight, Rough Day,* and *Run the Red Lights.* His poems have appeared in *The American Poetry Review, Best American Poetry, Harper's, New Republic, The New Yorker, Paris Review,* and *Poetry,* among other publications. He has been a Bread Loaf Fellow, a Lannan Foundation Marfa Residency Fellow, and writer-in-residence at George Washington University and Hugo House. He is a coordinator of the Idyllwild Arts Summer Writers Week and cohosts, with novelist J. Robert Lennon, the podcast *Lunch Box, with Ed and John.* He is a visiting writer at the University of Montana and lives in Portland, Oregon.

Poetry is vital to language and living. Since 1972, Copper Canyon Press has published extraordinary poetry from around the world to engage the imaginations and intellects of readers, writers, booksellers, librarians, teachers, students, and donors.

WE ARE GRATEFUL FOR THE MAJOR SUPPORT PROVIDED BY:

THE PAUL G. ALLEN
FAMILY FOUNDATION

the POINT
envision·enact·evolve

Anonymous

Jill Baker and Jeffrey Bishop

Anne and Geoffrey Barker

Donna and Matt Bellew

Diana Broze

John R. Cahill

The Beatrice R. and Joseph A. Coleman Foundation Inc.

The Currie Family Fund

Laurie and Oskar Eustis

Saramel and Austin Evans

Mimi Gardner Gates

Gull Industries Inc. on behalf of William True

The Trust of Warren A. Gummow

Carolyn and Robert Hedin

Bruce Kahn

Phil Kovacevich and Eric Wechsler

Lakeside Industries Inc.
on behalf of Jeanne Marie Lee

Maureen Lee and Mark Busto

TO LEARN MORE ABOUT UNDERWRITING
COPPER CANYON PRESS TITLES,
PLEASE CALL 360-385-4925 EXT. 103

WE ARE GRATEFUL FOR THE MAJOR SUPPORT PROVIDED BY:

Peter Lewis

Ellie Mathews and Carl Youngmann as The North Press

Larry Mawby

Hank Meijer

Jack Nicholson

Petunia Charitable Fund and adviser Elizabeth Hebert

Gay Phinny

Suzie Rapp and Mark Hamilton

Emily and Dan Raymond

Jill and Bill Ruckelshaus

Cynthia Sears

Kim and Jeff Seely

Dan Waggoner

Randy and Joanie Woods

Barbara and Charles Wright

Caleb Young as C. Young Creative

The dedicated interns and faithful volunteers
of Copper Canyon Press

The Chinese character for poetry is made up of two parts:
"word" and "temple." It also serves as pressmark for
Copper Canyon Press.

The poems are set in Hightower.
Book design and composition by Phil Kovacevich

CPSIA information can be obtained
at www.ICGtesting.com
Printed in the USA
JSHW012011030520
5419JS00003B/3